CHICAGO BOTANIC GARDEN

PORTRAIT OF A GARDEN

"To the attentive eye, each moment of
the year has its own beauty,
and in the same field, it beholds,
every hour, a picture which was never
seen before, and which shall never
be seen again."

—*Ralph Waldo Emerson*

GARDENS EVOKE a variety of emotions, and so many of them elevate the human spirit. When the Chicago Botanic Garden was founded more than a quarter century ago, its mission was to teach the lessons of nature and thereby illuminate our lives.

The photographs of this book reveal a place of splendid horticulture, displays of striking harmony, and feelings of unbridled freedom. This portrait also depicts a place that changes constantly. The Garden is colorful, peaceful, exhilarating, fragrant, historic, sometimes exotic, frequently wild, and always very much alive.

Bringing the mysteries of nature closer to people is the objective of all serious gardeners, and it is the true mission of the Chicago Botanic Garden. For many people, these mysteries help penetrate the meaning of life. Visitors sense this power, and it often leads them to a long and intimate relationship with the Garden.

A walk through the Garden inspires delight in its intricate and radiant performances. This delight leads to an awareness of the collaboration between human beings and the world of plants. For many, a relationship with the Garden culminates in a conviction that the natural world really is our salvation. The message is that plants and the elements sustaining them deserve our respect and active care. The Garden serves as a representative and symbol for all the common gifts of nature throughout the Chicago area and beyond.

Welcome!

"There was pasture enough
for my imagination."

—*Henry David Thoreau*

The Chicago Botanic Garden is a place of many moods and countless impressions. Across a landscape of lakes and islands modeled after Beijing's Garden of Perfect Brightness, 23 separate gardens are woven seamlessly on 385 acres. In a place that sometimes rings with the chords and arpeggios of the grand carillon, the Botanic Garden is a place of simple pleasures, such as daffodils rampant on a spring morning.

The flowers of spring (clock-wise from above): snowdrop (*Galanthus nivalis*), guinea hen flower (*Fritillaria melea-gris*), crown imperial (*Fritillaria imperialis* 'Rubra'), and waterlily tulips (*Tulipa kaufmanniana*).

Every spring, the Bulb Garden greets visitors with rich color and delicate form. On the opposite page, star magnolia (*Magnolia stellata*) collects the brightness and warmth of an early May morning as drifts of tulips and narcissi radiate across the garden's gentle knolls. Here, the horticulturist's art echoes nature's clear message: spring is no time for reticence.

" The hours when the mind is absorbed by beauty are the only hours when we truly live."

—*Richard Jefferies*

When the Botantic Garden opened in 1972, one objective of the Chicago Horticultural Society was to introduce a broader palette of plants to the Chicago area. From the surprising appearance of early bulbs such as Dutch crocus (*Crocus vernus* 'Remembrance') to the splendors of hybrid lilies (*Lilium* 'Creme de la Creme'), the Garden maintains year-round interest for active gardeners and casual visitors. Here, the brick path winds along the outskirts of the Rose Garden en route to other gardens, such as the Waterfall Garden and Sansho-En, a short walk distant but in many ways worlds apart.

Visitors to the Enabling Garden, above, can look out across the water to one of the finest views of the ever-changing landscape. With raised gardening beds, adaptable tools, and movable containers, the Enabling Garden was designed to demonstrate lifelong gardening techniques for people of all ages and abilities.

The Circle Garden, one of the newest gardens, was inspired by the old notion that an array of annuals can provide Midwest gardeners with endless combinations of color, form, and texture—brilliant, lively, and at moments suggesting an Impressionist painting.

The message of the Botanic Garden takes many forms, and it is transmitted in many ways. The Children's Garden is a vital resource for educational programs and provides a setting for experiencing the rewards of working in close contact with nature.

On a hillside between the Waterfall and Rose Gardens, the Dwarf Conifer Garden features more than 400 conifers, showing how a variety of evergreen species enhances all gardens even when space is limited.

14

" The earth's vegetation is part of a web of life in which there are intimate
and essential relations between plants and the earth, between plants
and other plants, between plants and animals."

—*Rachel Carson*

"I do not understand how anyone can live without some small place of enchantment to turn to."

—*Marjorie Kinnan Rawlings*

The English Walled Garden, made up of a series of smaller gardens, provides sensations of color, fragrance, sunlight, and even antiquity. Perennial poppies (*Papaver orientale* 'Princess Victoria Louise') and biennial hollyhocks (*Alcea rosea* 'Singles'), above and opposite, are old-fashioned favorites. On pages 18 and 19, extravagant texture characterizes both white rhododendrons (*Rhododendron catawbiense* 'Album') and silvery wormwood (*Artemisia absinthium* 'Huntington Garden'). Just beyond the walls, in the English Oak Meadow pictured on pages 16 and 17, the friendliest of annuals— black-eyed Susans (*Rudbeckia hirta* 'Indian Summer') and common sunflowers (*Helianthus annuus* 'Sunbright')— display colorful exuberance.

"The gifts of life are the earth's."

—Henry Beston

The Botanic Garden is deeply dedicated to teaching, and some of the most agreeable lessons are taught in the Fruit and Vegetable Garden. Rarely is the labor of the gardener or the teacher conducted to such reward. The garden's grape arbor (preceding page), for example, encourages both contemplation and cultivation. A kitchen garden includes heirloom vegetables not normally available, and the larger beds demonstrate maximum production by home gardeners. Happily, the culinary and floral arts merge in this garden, and by midsummer a plethora of lettuces vies with the attractions of plumed celosia for our attention.

Education takes a more serious, though hardly less relaxing, tone in the Heritage Garden. Here, horticulturists have organized a true encyclopedia of plants, largely the taxonomy devised by the great Carolus Linnaeus. Connections are sometimes surprising, as in the lily family bed, right, with *Hosta* and *Hemerocallis* varieties brought together in an instructive and lush composition of the gardener's art.

The pleasures of single flowers provide simple counterpoint to the striking rapture of whole gardens. And spring sometimes surprises with delicate perennials such as the Wonderland Iceland poppy (*Papaver nudicaule* 'Wonderland') and orrisroot iris (*Iris* x *germanica* var. *florentina*).

The Home Landscape Garden highlights the human touch in confined spaces not unlike the gardens of many homes. To the left, Prairie Song daylilies (*Hemerocallis* 'Prairie Song') are combined with the purple coneflower (*Echinacea purpurea*), a prairie native now known to have medicinal uses. To the right, a drapery of nasturtium (*Tropaeolum majus*) overflows its limestone terrace.

The glories of early summer include peonies (*Paeonia* 'Sea Shell'), but the Home Landscape Garden makes fine displays of quiet plants as well. Lemon daylilies (*Hemerocallis lilioasphodelus*) amid a variety of ferns show how discrete water features can inspire a range of garden ideas. Another possibility combines narrow-leaf cattails (*Typha angustifolia*) with waterlilies (*Nymphaea* 'Marliacea Albida') in the Blue Heron Pond.

Sculpture has always provided the gardens with architecture that endures through the lush seasons and the frozen ones. Above, "Otter Girl," Sylvia Shaw Judson's figure of a Celtic legend, defines the intimate space of the boxwood courtyard.

Sansho-En, Garden of Three Islands, was completed in 1982 as a stroll garden, with a nod to the Zen Buddhist objective of self-examination and enlightenment. This Japanese garden is a place of contemplation where the values of simplicity, change, contrast, and venerable age are embodied in an array of deliberate garden features. The varied profiles of stately pines are highlighted with the rhododendrons of spring and the maple's bright foliage in fall.

"Is this where we live, I thought, in this place at this moment, with the air so light and wild?"

—*Annie Dillard*

One objective of the Chicago Botanic Garden is to demonstrate the striking diversity of plants that flourish in the Midwest. In the Naturalistic Garden, golden alexander (*Zizia aurea*) represents one of hundreds of native flowers that once covered the Illinois prairie prior to the plow. Of a more formal nature, foxgloves (*Digitalis purpurea*) grace the Plant Evaluation Garden, where long-term tests are conducted to determine the suitability of new plants and cultivars for the Midwestern climate.

The Rose Garden achieves what is rare in such typically formal settings— a naturalistic impression within a highly evolved design. Shrub, heirloom, and antique roses blanket the arbors along the Rose Walk. Hybrid teas (clockwise from upper left) Gold Medal, Duet, and Medallion roses are among the 160 varieties whose subtleties of color and fragrance often dispatch visitors directly to a world of romantic sonnets.

Water provides opportunities for drama at the Botanic Garden, a landscape that includes eight lovely lagoons. The Sensory Garden, left, demonstrates horticulture's vast repertoire. This garden is designed to touch all the senses with the kind of performance that penetrates the spirit.

The water's edge is lined with unusual and distinctive species such as black tupelo (*Nyssa sylvatica*), right, in autumn.

"Now is the time of the illuminated woods...
every leaf glows like a tiny lamp;
one walks through their lighted halls
with a curious enjoyment."

—*John Burroughs*

"As we diminish our environment, both physically and in terms of
our attitude toward it, so we diminish our range of attention.
Half the beauties of the world are no longer seen."

—*John Hay*

The Garden changes almost
seamlessly from place to
place, habitat to habitat.
The Waterfall Garden was
created in 1988 with granite
from Wisconsin and plants
such as butterfly bush
(*Buddleja alternifolia*) and
cutleaf staghorn sumac
(*Rhus typhina* 'Laciniata'),
left, which not only comple-
ment the water but exult
in the chill Midwestern
autumn as well. In so many
ways, the hand of the
gardener works in splendid
concert with the harmonies
of nature. To the right,
a cluster of daylilies
brightens the headwaters
of a stream.

When trees are ablaze with color in fall— and the leaves of the white ash (*Fraxinus americana*) reach their dramatic peak— the Botanic Garden brings a poignant climax to the elaborate seasonal changes that characterize northern Illinois.

A splendid diversity is being restored to the Garden's 100 acres of oak and hickory woodlands. Amidst quiet trails, fiddleheads of ferns embrace white trillium (*Trillium grandiflorum*). And natives such as smooth Solomon's seal (*Polygonatum canaliculatum*) with wild columbine (*Aquilegia canadensis*) show that the delicate stirrings of spring merit our admiration and even reverence.

"A woodland in full color is awesome as a forest fire,
in magnitude at least; but a single tree is
like a dancing tongue of flame to
warm the heart."

—Hal Borland

In the monochromes of winter, there remain life, and form, and interest in the Garden.
The pleasures of the place are more subtle: the fresh tracks of a resident fox,
or the drapery of residual foliage in this dormant beech (*Fagus grandifolia*). But for
many horticulturists and visitors, the frozen months are when the imagination
is richest and the most vivid gardens are planned.

On the Garden's recreated prairie, late summer offers hairy aster (*Aster pilosus*), New England aster (*A. novae-angliae*), tall goldenrod (*Solidago altissima*), cordgrass (*Spartina pectinata*), and ironweed (*Vernonia fasciculata*), along with other native tallgrasses and wildflowers that once covered most of Illinois like a country quilt. Now prairies are all too rare, but preservation and the creation of plant communities like this one have introduced a new palette to gardeners and new vitality to plants including the sawtooth sunflower (*Helianthus grosseserratus*), below, with a monarch butterfly.

"The sunshine grew warmer and richer, new plants bloomed every day; the air became more tuneful with humming wings, and sweeter with the fragrance of the opening flowers."

—*John Muir*